G000230905

Tiggy

BOOKS BY MISS READ

Novels

Village School * Village Diary * Storm in the Village
Thrush Green * Fresh from the Country
Winter in Thrush Green * Miss Clare Remembers
Over the Gate * The Market Square * Village Christmas
The Howards of Caxley * Fairacre Festival
News from Thrush Green * Emily Davis * Tyler's Row
The Christmas Mouse * Farther Afield
Battles at Thrush Green * No Holly for Miss Quinn
Village Affairs * Return to Thrush Green * The White Robin
Village Centenary * Gossip from Thrush Green
Affairs at Thrush Green * Summer at Fairacre
At Home in Thrush Green * The School at Thrush Green
Mrs Pringle * Friends at Thrush Green * Changes at Fairacre
Celebrations at Thrush Green * Farewell to Fairacre
Tales from a Village School * The Year at Thrush Green
A Peaceful Retirement

Anthologies

Country Bunch * Miss Read's Christmas Book

Omnibuses

Chronicles of Fairacre * Life at Thrush Green
More Stories from Thrush Green
Further Chronicles of Fairacre * Christmas at Fairacre
Fairacre Roundabout * Tales from Thrush Green
Fairacre Affairs * Encounters at Thrush Green
The Caxley Chronicles * Farewell, Thrush Green
The Last Chronicle of Fairacre

Non-fiction

Miss Read's Country Cooking * Tiggy
The World of Thrush Green * Early Days (comprising
A Fortunate Grandchild & Time Remembered)

Tiggy

Miss Read

Illustrated by
CLARE DAWSON

This edition published in 2007
by Orion Books Ltd
Orion House, 5 Upper St Martin's Lane,
London WC2H 9EA
An Hachette Livre UK company

1 3 5 7 9 10 8 6 4 2

First published in Great Britain in 1971
by Michael Joseph Ltd

A CIP catalogue record for this book is available from the British Library.

ISBN 978 0 7528 8237 6

Typeset by Deltatype Ltd, Birkenhead, Merseyside
Printed in Great Britain by Clays Ltd, St Ives plc

The Orion Publishing Group's policy is to use papers that are natural, renewable and recyclable products and made from wood grown in sustainable forests. The logging and manufacturing processes are expected to conform to the environmental regulations of the country of origin.

www.orionbooks.co.uk

Contents

* * * *

To
Gwen and Edith
who first befriended Tiggy

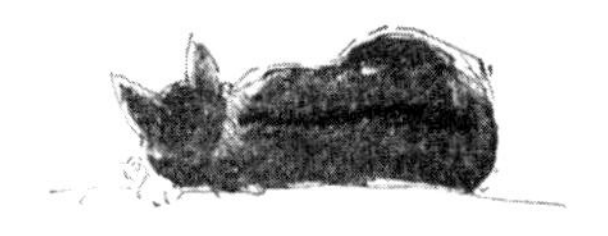

I The Last Cat

It all began during one of those long hot summers which are so rare in England.

The winter had been dreary and protracted, with the usual flurries of snow, slippery roads, fog and rain. But there had been nothing dramatic about it – no ten-foot drifts of snow to cut us off from the market town, no spectacular hard frosts forming a fringe of icicles along the thatched roofs. What we had endured was simply tedious coldness, dark mornings, and a remarkable dearth of winter sunlight.

We longed for the spring, and it took its time in coming that year. The daffodils and narcissi in the garden poked their green shoots through the soil, but refused to grow further in the coldness. The buds of the flowering currant – usually some of the earliest to break out in cheering fan-like leaf – remained sealed,

and the bare winter tracery of the trees continued in its nakedness until well on into March.

It must have been in that month that I woke one night to hear the caterwauling of love-sick cats. Certainly it was very cold as I shivered in my nightgown looking out of the bedroom window. Two black shapes raced squawking across the garden and disappeared from view, and I returned to bed again, remembering Timmy.

There has been a cat in the house for many, many years. Paddy was followed by Tinker when she died at fifteen years of age. Tinker, a noble tabby of great sagacity and bravery, lived until he was almost twenty.

It was not easy to replace such a lovable old warrior, but I had promised a young girl 'to save from the bucket' one of the many kittens born at her parents' farm in Oxfordshire.

'But it must be a tom-cat,' I stipulated. We had had a hair-raising experience, years before, with a spayed female, and I felt that I could face only a simple neutering operation.

We collected Timmy in the late summer. He was the only male, and pathetically frightened. His sisters were bonny fat lumps, and the farmer was most anxious for us to have one of these stronger specimens.

'We usually have much better kittens than that,' he told me, surveying the black and white scrap in the cat basket. But I was confident that Timmy would thrive, and we bore him home.

His first terrified dash, when he was released in the kitchen, was to sanctuary behind the refrigerator. With appalling difficulty he was rescued from the machinery underneath, and left with a warm blanket, an earth tray, minced meat and milk.

Not a sound was heard during the night, and next morning the meat and milk had gone.

At the sight of a human being, however, he fled

TIMMY

underneath the dresser, and virtually made his home there for three weeks. Fortunately, he cottoned on to the use of the earth tray, and emerged for this important function. But food and drink had to be put by the dresser, and he rarely approached it while people were about.

Time passed. He grew braver, and eventually discovered the garden, and liked to play and hide in a tall old hedge. Luckily, he seemed to ignore the road which runs by the cottage. Although this is an unclassified road, it carries a considerable amount of heavy traffic, and we knew the risk we were running when Timmy was adopted.

Before long the inevitable happened. One back leg was broken, presumably by a glancing blow from a vehicle. For six weeks, the poor kitten's leg was in plaster and strapped up to his chest while the bone knitted together, and for this period he was naturally immobile.

He became increasingly dear during these weeks. He had two cries. One for liver, which constituted the major part of his diet, and one for his earth tray. It was easy enough to push a saucer under his chin at mealtimes, but not so easy to support him over his earth tray, but it had to be done, and amazing though it may seem, there was never an accident throughout his period of immobility.

It was a great day when he was free from the plaster, and he could potter around the garden again. His distrust of the road was heartening. Now he turned left automatically from the cat-flap in the back door. It seemed as though Timmy could look forward to a ripe old age.

But it was not to be. A few months later, still weak no doubt, he picked up an infection, and died within a few days.

It was heart-breaking. He had had such a sad, brief life. We felt, somehow, that we had let him down, despite all our efforts.

'That's it!' we told each other, much shaken. 'Never again! It's simply not fair to bring a cat here while the traffic is so heavy. We must face the fact that *we can't have a cat*.'

And having sadly, but very sensibly, made our decision we settled down to being cat-less.

It was perfectly horrible.

The house seemed dead. There was no greeting when one returned home, no milk bowl on the kitchen floor, no cat-made dent in the eiderdown. Little kitchen tit-bits such as bacon rinds, giblets or fish skin, once put aside on old saucers for luscious cat-snacks, were now put out for the birds.

Friends were constantly offering kittens, each more adorable than the last. Heartrending tales of unwanted, homeless, misused cats had to be met with unnatural stoniness.

'That awful road!' we said.

'Certain death!' we said.

'Not fair to a cat!' we said.

'Never again!' we said.

We were wonderfully sure of ourselves.

2 Drought

The long cold months were bleaker than ever without a cat, but at last they passed. The cottage garden suddenly burst into life, fragrant with the heady scent of narcissi and daffodils.

The sun shone steadily. As the early spring bulbs faded, the lilac and laburnum brought their splendour, and the copper beech and ancient apple tree added to the gaiety.

We all revelled in the sunshine. This is downland chalky country, but a cap of heavy clay, some hundreds of acres in extent, covers the chalk hereabouts. Our little hamlet is situated upon this clay cap.

The heavy soil is difficult to work, cold and glutinous in wet weather. Gardeners reckon that crops here are three or four weeks behind the valley crops, for we are high too, and open to the winds.

But, of course, we score when there is a hot spell, for the heavy soil retains the moisture. When plants in the chalky gardens are drooping, ours are still thriving. And our roses take a lot of beating, for they relish the clay.

So, for many weeks, we enjoyed the dry weather, never doubting that rain would come before the gardens began to suffer.

But very little came. By July the clay was hard, and cracks had appeared in the borders and lawns. The bird bath was filled twice a day, and provided refreshment, not only for sparrows, finches, blackbirds, thrushes, robins and all the other friendly birds, but also for the bees which clung to the rim of the water, drinking thirstily.

It is a cruelly dry area in a drought. Older people in the village remember that a horse and cart spent the day going up and down the steep hill from the River Lambourn, some two miles away, fetching water for villagers, sheep, cattle, and the many farm horses. It was a great day when a deep bore was sunk in one of the gardens, and the inhabitants could fetch buckets of cold pure water from the chalk far below.

In the field opposite the cottage, the cows grazed. A galvanised water trough stood in one corner beneath the trees, and I noticed that it leaked. A large shallow puddle formed beside it, and this was the meeting place of the more timid birds, such as rooks and lapwings. Many a small animal, that hot summer, must have found refreshment there.

As the hot weather continued, I took to putting out a shallow bowl of water near the bird bath, and soon discovered that a hedgehog – perhaps more than one – visited it at night.

I am particularly fond of these little snuffling creatures and each night put out an old enamel plate, once the redoubtable Tinker's dinner dish, with bread and milk upon it.

First I soaked the bread well in warm water, squeezed it out, and then poured over a little milk. This rather Spartan fare appeared to be relished by the hedgehog, for every morning I collected an empty plate from the lawn, with growing elation.

'Look!' I'd say proudly. 'The hedgehogs have eaten the lot!'

'More likely a ghastly great rat,' was the comment one morning.

'Probably the birds,' said a neighbour. 'Have you actually *seen* the hedgehog?'

I had to admit that I had not. But there were certainly plenty of hedgehog droppings about, and I was confident that a Mrs Tiggywinkle, and relatives too, probably, enjoyed my parsimonious bounty. Later, I was to suffer pangs of remorse at the thought of that water bread, so frugally sprinkled with milk.

One evening about the end of July, my neighbour took her black Labrador dog for his usual evening walk. She crossed the road, and strolled down the edge of the field where the cattle trough stood. A row of fine old trees divides this field from the next, and beneath them runs some leafy undergrowth composed of various bushes, such as elder and blackberry interspersed with bracken, some dozen or so yards in width.

About halfway down, Nick the Labrador stopped to investigate the undergrowth. This was a spot about a hundred yards from the road.

A fierce hissing and spitting came from the bushes, and Nick was called to heel. He obeyed, but a few evenings later when he was taken that way again, he repeated his visit, only to be greeted with the same response. We know now that a cat with newly-born kittens was hidden there.

My cottage is one of three, each set in a roomy garden well furnished with trees and shrubs. Between the three of us, we must harbour scores of birds' nests in our thick hedges, and certainly plenty of moles, voles and field mice which live in holes beneath their shade.

The third cottage is not occupied continuously, but the owner is a keen fisherman and is there always during the trout fishing season and often at other times of the year. He is looked after by two maids – friends for many years – whose kitchen window overlooks the road and has a view of the row of trees where Nick had encountered the hidden source of the mysterious hissing.

On several occasions, about this time, they came down in the morning to find that the lid of the dustbin had been knocked off. The remains of meat-stained paper, well-chewed, were about, and it was plain that some desperately hungry animal was raiding the bin for any scraps, however unappetizing.

One morning, they saw a small black cat, with white feet, moving about under the cover of the hedge. She was pathetically thin and dusty, and her interest in the dustbin proved that she was the nightly marauder.

The kindly friends moved towards her to stroke her, but she backed away nervously. Obviously, she didn't trust human beings. They filled a saucer with milk and put it outside in the shade. They closed the door and watched from inside. Very soon, the cat appeared, and though nervous and anxiously alert, she lapped ravenously. It was quite apparent that she was almost starving.

Milk and food were put out regularly, and the cat became less timid. She let the friends approach her, and they saw that she was a mother cat, who had recently had kittens, and must be feeding a family somewhere nearby.

Two or three evenings later, they were lucky enough to see the family at play. It was an enchanting sight. There appeared to be five or six kittens, tabby, black, ginger – all tumbling about, sparring with each other, or making their wobbly way, small triangular tails erect, to suck milk from their mother who lay near them in the evening sunshine, watching their antics indulgently.

But the friends' delight in this pretty sight was mixed with anxiety. The family's hideaway was across the road – that road along which traffic pounded night and day. The mother must already cross it several times daily to eat and drink the good things put out at the back door.

How soon would it be before the kittens too discovered the saucers of food and followed their mother into danger?

It seemed that the mother cat's life, and that of her

babies, had been saved by the kindness of the two friends. But what of the future? If only she had found a home for them on the right side of that wretched road, they told each other anxiously.

They need not have worried.

The cat had summed up the situation perfectly.

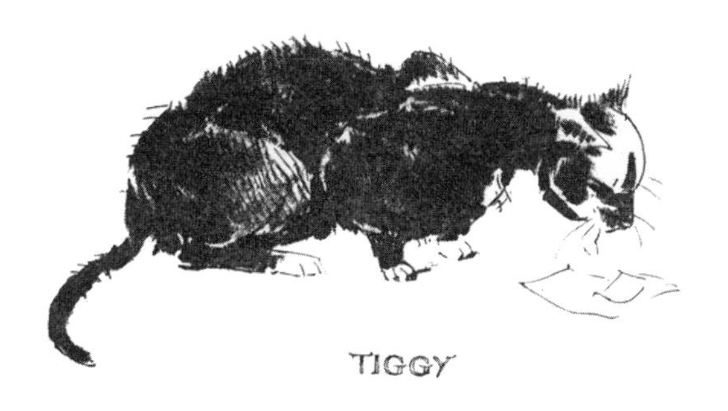

TIGGY

3 Mrs Tiggywinkle

Of course, we were all interested in the newcomers. I was never lucky enough to see the kittens at this stage, but Nick's mistress confirmed that the new home was some distance from their earlier one, which had been a hundred yards or so further down the hedge.

The present abode was strategically placed, from the cat's point of view. It was much nearer the source of food, a mere twenty yards or so from the bountiful back door. Moreover, it was very close indeed to the leaking cattle trough, and the large shallow puddle at which the mother cat could teach the kittens to lap. It must have been a godsend to them in that blazing summer.

Tall dry grass and thick undergrowth hid the babies from sight. She had provided for them beautifully, and she ruled them so strictly; it became clear that they were trained to stay under cover while she made her forays for food. Many a human parent could have profited by her example. She loved them well enough, but they must do as they were told, for their own safety.

She now began to visit my garden, and I fed her regularly. Here, I realised, was my hedgehog, my Mrs Tiggywinkle. Watching the poor little cat wolf down scraps, I thought remorsefully of that unpalatable moistened bread which she had been so pleased to devour.

She would not let me touch her, but purred as she ate, and seemed affectionate. By this time, she had grown brave enough to enter the friends' kitchen and let them pet her.

'She's obviously used to a house,' they told me. 'She likes to be inside, and "plucks cotton" on the rug and purrs all the time.'

A few days later, they discovered that the whole family had been brought across the road during the night, and were in their third home, hidden in the bushes near the back door, handy for the largesse.

Our admiration for this determined little cat grew as we thought about the planning and the work which had gone into all her manoeuvres.

This latest move had obviously been the most difficult one. The shift from the place of birth to the site near the water trough must have posed some problems, but it did not involve crossing the busy road. The kittens too, may have been small enough to be carried in her mouth to the second place. Nevertheless, they had to be carried one at a time, and meanwhile the others had been made to realise that they must stay put until fetched.

By the time the move across the road came, the kittens were too big to be carried. She must have shepherded them one at a time, when there were lulls in the flow of traffic, and made sure that the kittens on

each side of the road remained where they were told to remain. It probably took her all night to complete the operation. Later events support this supposition, as you shall hear.

Most of the time the kittens stayed hidden, but the two friends saw enough to realise that there were six altogether.

'Perhaps seven,' they said. 'There's another one much larger than the others – rather ugly, and a brownish colour. The mother cat doesn't seem to like it.'

We are fairly sure that this odd man out was one of an earlier litter, who had hung about in the neighbourhood, and was now hoping to attach himself to the new family and benefit from the food supplied from the cottages. The mother cat resented this and did her best to drive him away. No doubt she felt that it was time he fended for himself.

It so happened that, some weeks later, I saw a fine tom cat, with brindled fur like a hare's, climbing the lilac tree in my garden. It was intent on dislodging a lump of fat which I had hung there for the tits. It was, I decided, the odd man out, but later events gave me doubts, and so it proved.

Meanwhile, talking among ourselves, we pieced together what we knew of the black and white mother cat. She must have been living wild in the area for about eighteen months or two years, we reckoned, and had had one, or possibly two, earlier litters. Several cats had been sighted in the woods nearby and the hedges, and these might have been her descendants.

One mystery was certainly cleared up for me. Timmy had been much the same in looks – black with white feet. My neighbour told me that she had seen him sitting in our porch while we were out one day, but I knew this could not be so, because Timmy was still too frightened to emerge from the house at that time. Obviously, this little stray cat had sat there, and been seen.

It explained, too, the strange cat whom we had seen dash away from the porch on several occasions when we returned home at night. I think, now, that it was not only shelter she sought, but the proximity of human beings, nervous though she was at our approach. This cat, I feel sure, was once someone's pet.

I remembered, too, seeing this same cat leap up the grassy bank bordering the road. The car's headlights had turned her eyes to green fire, and her white feet made her even more conspicuous in the winter darkness.

Yes, it was quite plain that she had been in the neighbourhood for some time, fending for herself and her kittens, and coping with the dangers, not only of the road, but of other more powerful predators than herself, such as foxes.

She visited me regularly now for food, and occasionally let me stroke her while she was feeding. Her coat, once so dirty and rough, began to grow glossy again, her eyes brighter, her purr louder.

I was becoming very fond of her, and my respect for her as a mother grew daily. Nevertheless, I did not want the responsibility of owning her, nor the kittens I had never yet seen.

'I shan't let her indoors,' I said firmly. 'She can have her food regularly, and she can have a bed in the workshop for the winter, if she's still around then, but I'm not having her as an indoor pet. Think of all those kittens to come!'

'It's not fair to take on a cat here,' we said again.

'Not with that awful road,' we said.

'We learned our lesson with poor Timmy,' we said.

But we were, perhaps, a little less sure of ourselves.

'She's a fine little cat,' we agreed, watching her demolish her plateful of food.

'And quite able to look after herself, in the normal way,' we said, throwing a sop to our consciences. 'She probably wouldn't want to stay with us anyway.'

We watched her lick the empty plate, her eyes half-closed in bliss.

'Even if we could keep her,' we added. 'Which we can't, of course. Quite out of the question.'

Which only goes to show that you should never tempt Providence.

4 The Family Moves In

Two or three weeks passed. The weather remained hot and dry. The farmers were beginning to grumble at the lack of rain, gardeners were forbidden to use sprinklers on their parched lawns, and everyone's water-butt was empty.

The time came for the fisherman at the third cottage to return to his home. The two maids would be leaving too, and they were worried about the cat family who would look in vain for the food and drink which they had supplied so generously.

As the mother cat was coming regularly to me, I promised to continue to put out enough food and drink for all, and so they returned home with easier minds.

But, of course, with the house shut up, it was quite

clear that the cat would make another move. Where would she go this time, we wondered?

Although no one saw the move, she evidently returned across the road to the second home in the undergrowth, near the water trough. It still leaked, and a generous puddle gave the young family drinking water.

The mother continued to come daily for her food, but I still saw no sign of the kittens, although I walked across the road and peered several times among the bushes. Not so much as a squeak or rustle betrayed their presence. They had been well-disciplined, and warned against dangerous human beings.

One morning, about a week after the friends had returned home, Nick's mistress told me of the previous night's adventures.

'The mother cat brought them back across the road,' she said, 'one after the other, at about half-hourly intervals.' The night had been light, and she had watched the operation with enormous interest.

'The last kitten was tiresome and ran away up the road, but the mother sprinted after it, and headed it back.'

'And where did she take them?' I asked. I had a horrid feeling that I knew the answer already.

'I *think*,' said my neighbour, 'I *rather think* that she's put them all in your log shed!'

'Oh, no!' I cried in dismay. But at the same time I felt laughter bubbling inside. Trust a cat! Wasn't I the perfect person to land a cat family on? My neighbour already had a handsome ginger cat, Topper, and Nick the Labrador. My house was empty of animals, and food had been supplied regularly. Moreover, the log shed offered warmth, shelter and a perfect hiding place for the kittens. With her usual sagacity, the cat had put her plan into action.

And, it seemed, it had succeeded.

Or had it?

During the next two or three days, work was in progress by the open-ended log shed. We were putting down some paving stones at its entrance, and the noise and activity were considerable. Not once were the kittens in evidence. Not a whisker, not a tail, not a mew, not a hiss. Nothing.

'They *can't* be there,' I said. 'They wouldn't stay hidden for that length of time. Anyway we should have seen the mother lurking around. She must have taken them somewhere else. Perhaps into our hedge. They're certainly not in those logs.'

Still the cat appeared for her meals, but where from,

and where she went when they were demolished, I had no idea.

On the following Saturday I went to a fete. The weather was still glorious, and I returned in the golden evening well-content with the fun I had enjoyed.

Carefully, I backed the car into the garage, got out and then stood transfixed. Through the window of the garage I had a good view of the end of the log shed and the newly-placed flagstones.

There sat the mother cat with five adorable kittens playing round her. All the unworthy thoughts of getting the RSPCA man to capture and dispatch them humanely, vanished at once.

This was my first glimpse of the family, and I was immediately undone.

'We must never have a cat again,' did we say?

Well, we'd got six!

5 Strategy

It was no light problem to be shrugged off easily. Obviously, someone must accept responsibility for the family, and equally obviously the mother cat had decided I was the one to take them all on.

Certainly, it was no use turning a blind eye to the situation. By Christmas, if we allowed nature to take her bountiful course, we should be over-run with all the half-starved cats in the neighbourhood.

I decided that I would stop the supply at the source. The mother cat was now very tame and affectionate, even to the point of letting me pick her up and pet her. It should be fairly simple to put her into a basket, transfer her to the vet and get her spayed.

But when?

And what about the babies? They were still suckling,

although I reckoned that they must be five or six weeks old, but I knew that they could lap.

I rang up the vet and told him my six-fold troubles. After that reassuring conversation I felt my cares were halved.

'The first thing is to wean the kittens,' he told me. 'The mother's milk must dry up before we can operate. After about a fortnight bring her in.'

I doubled my order to the milkman and set to. There was a general demoting of dishes from occasional human use to daily kitten use, and a large pie-dish stood permanently filled with milk, on the flagstones.

To begin with, they would not venture forth if I were in sight, but by hiding behind a tree I was able to get a good look at the babies when they slowly emerged from the logs to lap.

There were certainly only five. One, I learned, had strayed into the road one night, from their home in the hedge, and been injured. Despite the care lavished on it all through the night by a young man in the village, it had to be dispatched the next day, as its jaw was broken and it was unable to feed.

The five that were left were fine specimens. Two were ginger and white, one a very dark tortoiseshell, one a pale clearly-marked tabby, and the biggest was black and white. The large outcast was not to be seen. Evidently, he had been successfully driven away by the mother, although he remained in the neighbourhood.

I saw him very occasionally, as dusk fell, looking round the garden for any tit-bits put out for the birds. But it was obvious that he had ceased to throw in his lot with this family, and he did not linger when he saw us about.

Their appetites were prodigious. Besides milk, they cleared saucers full of minced meat, gravy, fish, and tinned food. But the largest appetite of all belonged to the mother, and I had to carry her back to the house to make sure the kittens had their chance. There was no pretty standing back or 'children first' attitude on her part. If she got there first, she ate it. It was as simple as that.

I still fed her at the house, and now that she was going to become one of the household I decided that she must have a name. I pondered as I watched her piling onto the cheapest tinned cat food obtainable, set on Tinker's old enamel plate – the same one which had held the hedgehogs' nightly bread and milk.

Well, here was my hedgehog – my Mrs Tiggywinkle. What more suitable name could there be? She should be Tig, or Tiggy. An added advantage would be that if I called 'Timmy' or 'Tinker', in moments of mental aberration, then both names were near enough to Tiggy to be accepted.

The sun continued to shine, and I lodged two wooden seed boxes on the logs so that the kittens could have somewhere to sleep and sunbathe. Old sacks were folded and put into them for their bedding. I put two boxes ready, for I could not imagine that five such fat lumps and Tiggy could squeeze into one.

But when I approached stealthily in the mornings, I usually managed to see all six heaped up together before they caught sight of me and the five young ones fled into the interior. Tig, of course, was too interested in the dishes I carried to flee away.

I dreaded the day of Tiggy's spaying for several reasons. Should I be able to catch her? How would she stand the ten-mile journey? She had always been free. Even now, she didn't want to stay for long inside a house. How would she react to a small basket, inside a closed car?

And what about leaving her kittens? She would fight like a tiger to get back to them, I felt sure. And how would the kittens fare? Would they wander out to find her, and get lost? Would rats attack them in the night if Tiggy were not there to defend them?

But it just had to be done. When the day came, Tiggy was affronted at the meagre drop of milk which was all that she was allowed for a pre-operative breakfast. She drank it resignedly, let me pick her up, and within a minute she was in the basket while I strapped the wire door shut with shaking fingers.

She seemed more bewildered than frightened, and I put her into the car with little trouble, and set off.

Then it began. The most unearthly squallings drowned the noise of the engine. When these stopped, she began a determined assault on the door, thrusting her black muzzle through a small gap at the top, and nearly giving me heart-failure at the wheel. If she managed to get her head through, the top of the door would probably snap back and trap her neck, and she would be throttled.

On the other hand, if I stopped to extricate her, she might escape into the car and I should assuredly be lacerated to the bone at some stage or other. I made all possible speed to the surgery, uttering soothing noises which were rightly ignored by the outraged cat.

'Call back about six,' they told me at the surgery when I handed over the baleful Tig. I felt a traitor. Mothering was Tiggy's supreme accomplishment, and I was callously robbing her of it.

On the other hand, I told myself, as I drove home to the temporary orphans, wasn't it better to have one cheerful spayed cat than one permanently pregnant one and a growing horde of unwanted kittens?

Lord knows, I thought, as I chopped up revolting raw liver in my role as temporary nursemaid, five were more than enough!

6 Nursemaid To Five

It was a very different Tiggy I collected at six o'clock. She lay still and quiet, in a drugged sleep, in the basket. A large, bare, grey patch showed the scar of the operation on her side.

'She'll come round in a few hours,' they assured me. 'By the way, keep her away from the kittens for a week.'

What a hope, was my private thought! However, I promised to do my best, and we returned home to put the sleeping cat in the workshop near the house. The basket door was left open, and a seed-box bed filled with fresh hay stood beside it. Milk, water and an earth tray were left for the invalid, and we went to bed and slept fitfully.

Rats the size of goats invaded the log shed in my dreams. Occasionally, a kitten-eating snake entered, too, with one or two foxes and mad dogs for good measure. It was quite a relief to get up and see for myself, when at last morning came.

There was the usual diving for cover when I arrived at the log shed, but one of the ginger and white ones remained in the seed box. She watched me put down the plates, but would not let me stroke her. Nevertheless, it was progress.

I went to the workshop to see if Tiggy were awake. She was curled up in the hay, but roused herself when I went in. I need not have feared that my treachery would antagonise her. She was more affectionate than ever, rubbing her head against me, and as pleased as ever to see food.

She was still bemused and, after eating, fell asleep again. She slept most of that day, while I kept an anxious eye on the log shed, and put down dishes of milk and food for my charges.

In the evening, Tiggy awoke, and as I entered the workshop, she neatly dodged around my legs and escaped. I expected her to run straight to the kittens, but to my surprise she followed me to the kitchen, looking for food. This proved something which I had long suspected. Food came first with Tiggy, children second, good mother though she was.

Having eaten a hearty meal, she was returned to her

sick-quarters and seemed to settle down for the night. Had she forgotten the kittens, I wondered?

I viewed the possibility of acting nursemaid to five kittens, with some dismay. Nevertheless, I remembered the vet's light-hearted advice about keeping mother and kittens apart for a week. Who knows? It might be possible if things continued in this vein.

The next morning Tiggy was nowhere to be seen in the workshop. It was impossible for her to get out.

Dumbfounded, dish in hand, I surveyed the many possible hiding places. There were plenty. Stacked deckchairs, one or two old baskets, a pile of wood and two or three large cardboard boxes, all offered cover, but as I stood there, wondering where to look first, a mew came from the topmost shelf close to the ceiling. There, among the paint pots, squatted Tiggy.

To have climbed up there was a considerable feat for any cat. For Tiggy, never particularly agile and with a newly-sewn operation scar, it was a sign of her determination to escape.

I helped her down and took her into the house to feed her. As soon as the meal had gone, she made for the door. She was herself again, and had remembered the kittens.

For an hour or so, I did my best to distract her attention, but the position was hopeless. At last, I let her out – vet or no vet – and she hustled off purposefully to the log shed. I followed her, at a distance, and watched the reunion.

It was well worth seeing. Tiggy made little chirruping noises as she approached the flagstones, and out of the logs tumbled the kittens. They rubbed their heads

round Tiggy and before long she had settled down in the sunshine, surrounded by the family, and began to give each one a thorough wash. Obviously, I had fallen down badly on this part of kitten care.

I returned to the house, glad to hand over some of my duties to Tiggy, but apprehensive about any accidental damage or infection of the scar.

I need not have worried. All the cats flourished, and now began an amusing phase of the kitten-rearing.

As soon as Tiggy heard me about, first thing in the morning, she appeared for food. Usually I took the kittens' dish up to the flagstones whilst she fed in the kitchen. This gave them a chance to have a meal before their mother found it.

Sometimes I was too busy cooking my own breakfast and putting down Tiggy's to go to the log shed immediately. The kittens' meal would have to wait a while.

But this did not suit Tiggy. As soon as her own hunger was satisfied, she hurried back to the log shed to see that the babies had been supplied. And if they had not, then back she bustled, in a very determined fashion, to let me know that I was slipping in my duties.

She mewed plaintively until I carried the food to the

flagstones, and waited to see me put it down before making the particular chirruping sound which brought them forth from their hiding places. There was no doubt about it, Tiggy now looked upon me as a mother's help, and one who needed a pretty firm hand, too, if the job were to be properly done.

7 The Wily Brood

And so we settled down to a rough and ready routine. Luckily, we were not going away that summer so that the kittens had most of our attention.

The next problem was to find homes, and this meant, of course, taming them enough to accept human beings as friends.

This was a daunting task, I knew, and I was given no encouragement by well-intentioned friends, who assured me lugubriously that it was absolutely impossible to expect kittens born in such circumstances to become really domesticated.

I was inclined to believe them. Certainly, Tiggy's training was going to be difficult to undo. She ruled them with a rod of iron, and one of the first rules they had learnt was to keep away from human beings.

She kept a sharp eye on their playing places, too.

They were allowed to play only within a few yards of their home, but she showed them how to climb an old plum tree, close at hand, and taught them how to hunt at night. There were plenty of gruesome remains on the flagstones in the morning, and I noticed how sharply the kittens watched the birds in the hedges.

She refused to let them come near the house, looking upon it, I believe, as her own particular preserve, a place of refreshment, and a haven from the cares of motherhood.

Once or twice, we saw them following her across the lawn to the house, but each time she chased them back, cuffing them severely if they gave trouble. It did one's heart good to see such firm parental discipline!

Nevertheless, it made my own task much more difficult. How could I get these babies to trust me, and other human beings? It was no good expecting people to give homes to kittens as wild as these were. In any case, I could not hope to catch them at this stage.

The only thing to do was to accustom them to human society, and to win their trust with food and affection, in that order!

It was plain that the task was going to be formidable. I was the only one willing to make advances. The five kittens were resolutely anti-social and fled at my approach. An occasional paw or tail could be seen through the chinks of the logs, but these remained motionless and unresponsive.

It was a daunting outlook.

I took to spending hours sitting perched on a good stout log on the flagstones. Beside me was a plate of tempting food, such as morsels of raw liver, to help my endeavours.

It was not as arduous as it sounds. The sun streamed down very pleasantly there in the mornings, and I quite

enjoyed idling my time away waiting for kittens to appear. I kept up a flow of encouraging noises. After all, they had to get used to the human voice, and to associate it, I hoped, with food and stroking.

It was a long job. The first to succumb to blandishment was one of the little ginger and white ones. She had always been the last to flee, and always looked slightly sleepy, so that she was known as 'the dopey one'. After a week or so, she let me stroke her head as she fed.

The others were less amenable. It took over a week of patient sitting and talking before they would all venture forth. Even then, they approached the dish very warily, ready to dash back among the logs if I moved.

Gradually, I encouraged them to take morsels of meat from my hand. All this took a great deal of time, but it was most encouraging to see them becoming tamer as the weeks passed.

One morning, Dopey looked even dopier than usual. She sat still and shivered, and I transferred her, without any struggling on her part, to another box of hay which I put in the closed end of the shed, where she would have more shelter.

It was plain that she was ill, and I put Tiggy in with

her, propping open the door so that she could visit the other kittens easily.

She was very solicitous towards the little invalid, washing her gently and curling up in the hay with her for the night. I made up my mind to see the vet if the kitten were no better in the morning.

But the vet was not needed, for when I looked into the shed the next morning Dopey lay dead. Tiggy, roused from sleep, seemed quite unconcerned, and came back to the house with me for her breakfast.

Her appetite, despite this family bereavement, remained unimpaired, and poor little Dopey was buried in the shrubbery near Tinker and Timmy.

8 Good Homes Wanted

It was now the end of September, some five or six weeks since my first glimpse of the kittens, and they were all quite big enough to leave their mother if only homes could be found for them and – even more important – if we could catch them!

Of course, I envisaged the ideal home for my charges. It should be well away from busy roads, with grass to play in and nibble and trees to climb. Then, too, for such timid kittens, it would be best if each were the only pet in the household. Preferably there should be no young children who might mishandle them through ignorance. I have seen too many kittens, gripped in over-loving hands, who, when they retaliated with a scratch, were punished unfairly.

The prospective owners I intended to see. I was not

going to part with a kitten which might be passed on elsewhere to an unknown and, possibly, cruel fate.

No, it must be *a good home*, in every sense of the word, providing affection, proper care, food, space and warmth.

It would not be easy. I might be forced to compromise, but those were my standards, and I was lucky enough, when the time came, to be able to keep to them with only minor adjustments.

I must have asked dozens of people if they would like a kitten. Either they had one already, or had promised to have one, or they had a dog which would devour a kitten on sight, or one of the family was allergic to fur, or the traffic was a hazard, or they just simply hated cats!

Heavens, how I worked! It really looked, at one stage, as if all my efforts to prepare the kittens for domesticity were doomed to failure.

The first gleam of hope came from my hairdresser who listened to my tale of anguish and said calmly: 'I'll have one for my sister. Is there a black and white one?'

There was indeed – the finest of the remaining four – and he was now ear-marked for a perfect home. Luckily, too, he was now as tame as Dopey had been, and allowed us to stroke him.

Although I knew that there was a little boy of two, called Richard, in the household, I had no fears for the kitten's mishandling. He was already a cat-lover, and had been trained by his wise mother to be very gentle with animals. I felt pretty sure that these two would grow up together very happily.

One evening a week or so later, I put down a trail of liver across the flagstones to the open cat basket, and the black and white kitten obligingly walked in.

He stood the journey equably, and was introduced into his new home. I thought about him often that night, and hoped he would settle down away from his mother and the rest of the family. How would he like being in a house, I wondered, after being so free?

I was told the next day that this mite from the backwoods spent his first evening sitting on the couch in his new home, watching television. George – for that was to be his name – was obviously an adaptable cat.

I have weekly bulletins on his progress. He has an enormous appetite, and obviously takes after his mother in this respect. He takes a keen interest in Richard's model cars, and in the cat next door, called William, whose food he eats as well as his own. George certainly fell on his feet.

Another cat-loving friend came to the rescue. He put

up a notice in the local bank where he works, and through this kind effort two more homes were found.

Two newly-married young girls came to inspect the kittens one evening. There were now only three to choose from: the second ginger and white one, the dark tortoiseshell, called Smokey, and the light stripey one.

We stood, strategically placed behind a hedge, to watch them feed. The prospective owners were delighted with the sight, and made their choice.

'If I can catch the right one,' I was obliged to stipulate. 'Or any of them, for that matter!'

Both were happy to co-operate. If I could not catch the right kitten for each, then whichever was delivered would be welcome, they assured me. As for sex, they were quite happy to let the vet sort out that little matter when the time came.

They could not have been kinder, and I was greatly relieved. Good homes – really good homes – for three!

'There's just one thing,' said one of the girls as we returned to the house. 'A stray cat comes to my house and I feed it. I hope it will get on with this new kitten.'

We easily brushed aside the visiting stray, in our present carefree mood, and promised to deliver the kittens in about three weeks' time.

I soon realised that I should have taken the stray cat

more seriously. After all, I had plenty of experience with strays by this time.

A few days later, the girl telephoned in some distress. 'That cat,' she said distractedly, 'has just moved in *with a kitten*! I shall simply have to adopt them. Can you find another home for yours?'

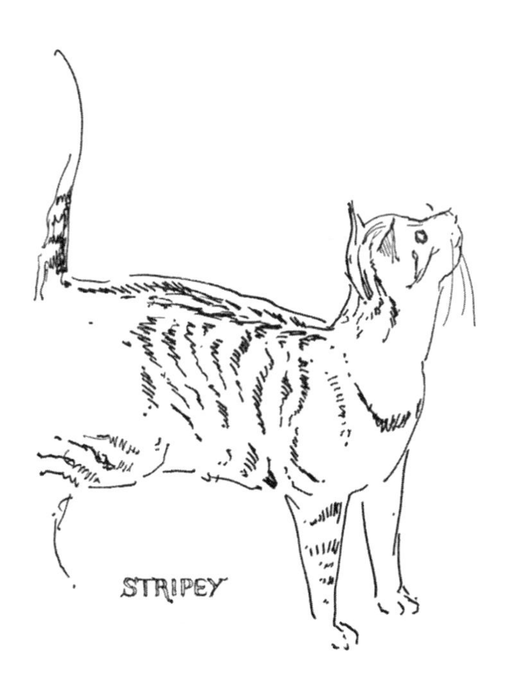

I knew exactly how she felt. So recently had I suffered the same dismay and helplessness. I assured her that my kitten would either stay here or be found a home, and we parted with mutual sympathy.

But I was particularly sorry about this set-back, for this kitten's home would have been ideal – a cottage set well back from the road, in commonland thick with bracken, a cat's idea of heaven! But it was not to be.

It was comparatively easy to catch the remaining ginger and white kitten and to transport her to her new home, which was a modern house on a new estate. She would be the only pet. There was a garden, and plenty of open grassy places in front of the houses. The new owner was used to cats and a true cat-lover, and I felt sure that this kitten would be very lucky.

But her release in the new home was anything but tranquil. She horrified us all by dashing wildly about the room, until at last, exhausted, she took refuge behind a curtain.

I was extremely worried about this kitten, but was relieved to hear from another friend that she gradually settled down.

And so we were left with two kittens. One was the tabby, which we called 'the stripey one', and Smokey, the dark tortoiseshell. Both were decidedly frisky, and tore away into the neighbours' gardens whenever we approached.

Stripey was a particular favourite of mine – beautifully marked, with here and there a touch of ginger among the clear tabby stripes. A home awaited him in a quiet road in the local market town.

'He's still quite wild,' I told the couple anxiously.

They were unperturbed. 'Our last cat was completely crazy,' they told me comfortingly, and obviously it had flourished happily with them for many years. It was plain that Stripey would be going to an understanding home.

We arranged a day for his delivery. I was confident that this one was male, although I had told the prospective owners cautiously that I did not know to which sex Stripey belonged, and they were game to take the chance.

He really was adorable. I sometimes came upon him washing his small face, or climbing the old plum tree

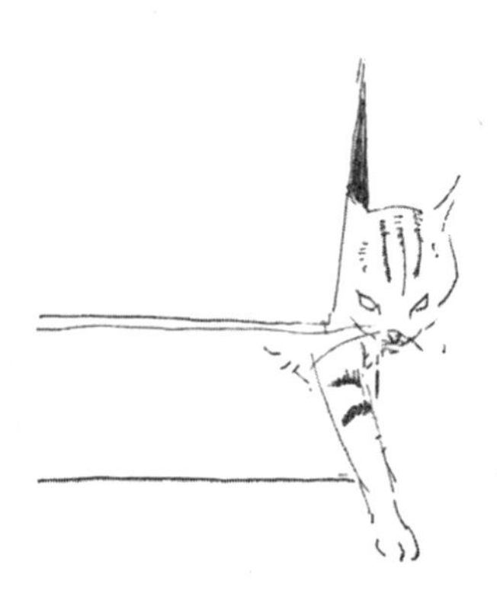

with Smokey, who was by far the most adventurous climber of the family.

The two were inseparable. Smokey was wilder than Stripey, if anything, and now that the two were so much together they seemed to grow more independent, and wary of my overtures.

On the evening of Stripey's move, I repeated my usual strategy of a liver trail, but Stripey would have none of it. I think, looking back, that he saw us put one of the other kittens into the basket and carry it to the car. He wasn't going to have anything to do with that contraption!

The next morning we went apologetically to the house and confessed that we had been beaten. We would try again.

We tried many times during the next two weeks, and always the result was the same. Stripey and Smokey took one look at us as we approached, and dashed away across the gardens to cover.

We were utterly defeated.

Sadly, full of apologies, we had to tell the prospective owners that it was hopeless, and that some tamer, luckier kitten must be sought for by them. They were very understanding, and I only hope that they finally found a more amenable cat.

It looked now as though we must face having three

cats on the establishment. Tiggy had now settled in well, sitting on our laps, curling up on the sunniest bed, and generally behaving as though she had lived with us for years.

She revelled in the warmth and comfort of a house, and showed her appreciation with a display of affection which was touching.

The weather was now becoming chilly. The leaves were tumbling down from the trees, and the first frosts arrived. The logs were beginning to be used, and we put a cat-flap on the workshop door, nearer the house. This was a strong weatherproof building which would provide warmth and shelter for the two half-grown cats who were still too scared to come indoors.

I took to putting their food and drink in there, and provided two seed-box beds stuffed with hay.

They quickly learned to push up the cat-flap, and each morning there were hollows in the hay beds where they had slept.

This state of affairs continued for several weeks, and then one morning a tragedy occurred.

Smokey's body was found on the grass verge outside the cottage. She had obviously been run down by a vehicle and from the nature of the injuries, she must have died instantly.

Stripey definitely missed his companion during the

next few days and wandered about, mewing pitifully. He took to running to Tiggy whenever she appeared, and although she was kind, in an off-hand way, she did not encourage him to come indoors.

Now that he was bereft and the weather was becoming so cold, I decided to let Stripey share the house with his mother. It was pretty plain, by this time, that we were destined to keep Stripey as well as Tiggy, and certainly we were so attached to him that we could not have parted from him easily after all our vicissitudes together.

He took to coming into the kitchen for his food, and now that Smokey had gone, he seemed readier to accept human companionship. Naturally, the cold weather helped our efforts, and very soon he ate regularly indoors, and found that the hearthrug in front of the stove was the perfect place for comfort.

Tiggy resented his presence strongly. She growled whenever he came in, and did her best to drive him away. It says much for Stripey's spirit that he bravely resisted her attacks, but he had to put up with many a cuff and spit.

It took some weeks before Tiggy accepted the inevitable and let him settle in on equal terms. Even now, she chooses the best spot in the room, and Stripey has to make do with what is left.

Tiggy is quite aware that she is the top cat, and we are only too ready to accept the situation. After all, she has worked hard enough for her position.

9 The Two Who Stayed

Stripey was now six months old and the right age to be neutered.

It was comparatively easy to catch him now that he was indoors, and we set out with a yowling basket of furious cat one January day.

'Male or female?' the girl had asked me when I rang up to make an appointment.

'No idea,' I told her cheerfully.

We delivered Stripey to the vet's care and went home to prepare the workshop as a temporary convalescent home again.

'One thing,' we told each other, 'it's a much simpler operation for a male.'

We thought again.

'If Stripey is a male,' we added.

As we might have guessed, Stripey was a female,

despite her boyish looks and behaviour. She spent two days as a pampered patient and then romped back to normality, only the scar showing any sign of invalidism.

An interesting thing was that her fur took almost twice as long as Tiggy's to grow thick enough to cover the scar. Certainly, her fur is softer and finer than her mother's, but Tiggy was operated on in September when her winter coat was about to grow. This may have been one reason for the difference in time.

Incidentally, it was on the occasion of Stripey's first outing after her operation, as she was pottering vaguely about the lawn, that I saw the large brindled tom cat for the last time. Bolder than he had ever been, he appeared at dusk and made amorous advances to the somewhat surprised Stripey.

He rolled about seductively, giving strident love-sick cries. Fearful of any harm to Stripey's new scar, we chased her suitor away, and brought the lady indoors.

'Just in time!' was my first thought, congratulating myself on having the operation safely over. But I heard later that this is quite a common occurrence. A newly-spayed female attracts the male just as if she were on heat.

What became of the tom cat, whom we thought of as the outcast, we do not know. He was a splendid animal, magnificently strong, and he may have moved away to another territory where he could be king. Or he may have met a sad end on this dangerous stretch of road, as so many more have done.

But there is yet another development. Recently, a small brindled female cat, so strange-looking with her large pointed ears and sharp muzzle that she has been nicknamed 'Foxy' by my neighbour, has appeared and produced four fine kittens. She too has been befriended by the two kind-hearted maids. Could this be the big outcast kitten who tried so hard to join Tiggy's younger ones, and is now repeating family history? We shall never know.

Tiggy and Stripey have now settled down together very affectionately. If anything, Tiggy is the more playful, starting the evening fight which they both enjoy. They greet each other with much head-rubbing and mutual washing when they meet, and have even become so accommodating as to share one plate of food.

We little realised how fond we should become of Tiggy and her family. That first shock of dismay when we found that we were to be their unwilling hosts fast changed to admiration and devotion.

We have learnt a lot in these last few months, which is why I thought it worthwhile to record these true events. For one thing, it seems that kittens, however wild, do respond to companionship – with the help of food, of course.

The response varies, naturally. I feel quite sure that Smokey would never have become as tame as Tiggy is now. I doubt if Stripey will ever be quite as relaxed and demonstrative as her mother but she is, nevertheless, a charming household pet. I think we have proved that it is possible to tame such young wild ones, despite the gloomy prognostications of our friends who, I think, doubted our sanity when coming upon us at our lonely vigils by the logs.

But we have learned most of all from Tiggy herself. One cannot help marvelling at the courage and ingenuity of that starving little mother cat who set out to overcome all the obstacles in her path to provide for her family, and triumphed superbly.

Her success has brought great happiness to us all, and it is to Tiggy that we make our final salute.